A Taste of Scotland

The essence of Scottish cooking, with 30 classic recipes
shown in 100 evocative photographs

Carol Wilson & Christopher Trotter

LORENZ BOOKS

This edition is published by Lorenz Books, an imprint of Anness Publishing Ltd, Hermes House, 88–89 Blackfriars Road, London SE1 8HA; tel. 020 7401 2077; fax 020 7633 9499

www.lorenzbooks.com; www.annesspublishing.com

If you like the images in this book and would like to investigate using them for publishing, promotions or advertising, please visit our website www.practicalpictures.com for more information.

UK agent: The Manning Partnership Ltd; tel. 01225 478444; fax 01225 478440; sales@manning-partnership.co.uk
UK distributor: Grantham Book Services Ltd; tel. 01476 541080; fax 01476 541061; orders@gbs.tbs-ltd.co.uk
North American agent/distributor: National Book Network; tel. 301 459 3366; fax 301 429 5746; www.nbnbooks.com
Australian agent/distributor: Pan Macmillan Australia; tel. 1300 135 113; fax 1300 135 103; customer.service@macmillan.com.au
New Zealand agent/distributor: David Bateman Ltd; tel. (09) 415 7664; fax (09) 415 8892

Publisher: Joanna Lorenz
Editors: Joy Wotton and Jennifer Mussett
Photographer: Craig Robertson
Food Stylist: Emma MacIntosh
Prop Stylist: Helen Trent
Designer: Nigel Partridge
Production Controller: Claire Rae

ETHICAL TRADING POLICY

At Anness Publishing we believe that business should be conducted in an ethical and ecologically sustainable way, with respect for the environment and a proper regard to the replacement of the natural resources we employ.

As a publisher, we use a lot of wood pulp to make high-quality paper for printing, and that wood commonly comes from spruce trees. We are therefore currently growing more than 500,000 trees in two Scottish forest plantations near Aberdeen – Berrymoss (130 hectares/320 acres) and West Touxhill (125 hectares/305 acres). The forests we manage contain twice the number of trees employed each year in paper-making for our books.

Because of this ongoing ecological investment programme, you, as our customer, can have the pleasure and reassurance of knowing that a tree is being cultivated on your behalf to naturally replace the materials used to make the book you are holding.

Our forestry programme is run in accordance with the UK Woodland Assurance Scheme (UKWAS) and will be certified by the internationally recognized Forest Stewardship Council (FSC). The FSC is a non-government organization dedicated to promoting responsible management of the world's forests. Certification ensures forests are managed in an environmentally sustainable and socially responsible way. For further information about this scheme, go to www.annesspublishing.com/trees

Material in this book has been previously published in *Scottish Heritage Food and Cooking*

NOTES

Bracketed terms are intended for American readers.

For all recipes, quantities are given in both metric and imperial measures and, where appropriate, in standard cups and spoons.

Follow one set of measures, but not a mixture, because they are not interchangeable.

Standard spoon and cup measures are level. 1 tsp = 5ml, 1 tbsp = 15ml, 1 cup = 250ml/8fl oz.

Australian standard tablespoons are 20ml. Australian readers should use 3 tsp in place of 1 tbsp for measuring small quantities.

American pints are 16fl oz/2 cups. American readers should use 20fl oz/2.5 cups in place of 1 pint when measuring liquids.

Electric oven temperatures in this book are for conventional ovens. When using a fan oven, the temperature will probably need to be reduced by about 10–20°C/20–40°F. Since ovens vary, you should check with your manufacturer's instruction book for guidance.

The nutritional analysis given for each recipe is calculated per portion (i.e. serving or item), unless otherwise stated. If the recipe gives a range, such as Serves 4–6, then the nutritional analysis will be for the smaller portion size, i.e. 6 servings. Measurements for sodium do not include salt added to taste.

Medium (US large) eggs are used unless otherwise stated.

Front cover shows Strawberry Cream Shortbreads – for recipe, see page 56.

contents

introduction

Scotland's magnificent culinary heritage has a long and illustrious history. The flavours of Scottish cuisine reflect a rugged, hardy landscape. The heather-clad moors and dense forests that covered much of the land ensured a plentiful supply of fresh game; the seas, rivers and lochs teemed with fish; beef, dairy cattle and sheep thrived in pastures; all kinds of wild fruits, berries and aromatic herbs were gathered from fields and hedgerows; while the cold, wet climate proved ideal for oats and barley. In the past, oatcakes were a

part of almost every meal, and Scottish shortbread and bannocks are renowned throughout the world.

The wild mushrooms and berries complement the rich game meats for which Scotland is famed such as venison, wild boar and grouse. The smokehouses add a sumptuous taste to herring, salmon, trout and haddock, resulting in such local delicacies as Arbroath smokies and Loch Fyne kippers.

Left: Scotland is often divided into three regions: the rugged Highlands, busy Lowlands and remote Islands.

Above: Life in the Highlands relied upon wild deer for venison and the rivers and lochs for salmon.

The national cuisine

Scottish cuisine has been shaped by its geography and climate but also by social, cultural and political events. The cooking is interwoven with Scotland's turbulent history – the threads producing a tapestry of flavours and culinary traditions.

Over the centuries foreign invaders and settlers, particularly those from Scandinavia, had a powerful effect on Scotland's developing cuisine.

The Vikings taught the Scots how to make use of the rich wealth of the seas. Trade with overseas markets introduced new ingredients such as spices, sugar, dried fruits and wines to the Scottish kitchen. Politics too had a major role: the Auld Alliance with France, intended to curb the dynastic ambitions of English monarchs, had a great and lasting effect on the national gastronomy. All these influences brought new foods, cooking methods, ideas and skills, which over time became part of a colourful culture based on high-quality Scottish produce.

Below: Even today, Scotland's many fine restaurants rely on local sources for their excellent fish and shellfish.

Above: Oatmeal porridge with fresh cream is a popular Highland dish.

Whisky distilleries

Acknowledged as Scotland's national drink, whisky – in the Gaelic, *uisge beatha*, meaning the water of life – has been produced for centuries as a way of using up rain-soaked barley after a wet harvest. Single malt whisky is made from malted whisky in pot stills. The whisky industry is now one of the country's biggest earners, bringing in hundreds of millions of pounds each year. Scotland produces outstanding malt, grain and blended whiskies. Many of the best-known quality distilleries are still owned by the family or clan that began making the whisky centuries before.

Traditional favourites

The Scots are careful to preserve their time-honoured heritage dishes. Aberdeen Angus beef, Highland game, Tayside berries, salmon and other fish and shellfish and of course Scotch whisky are recognized as the finest in the world. Haggis is still widely made and is often served with 'neeps and tatties' (turnips and potatoes). Every region has its own specialities, such as Cullen Skink, Orkney, Ulslay and Galloway cheeses, Edinburgh rock, Dundee cake and a host of other much-loved local delicacies.

Below: True Highland coffee uses a Highland or Island malt whisky, such as Laphroaig or Dalwhinnie.

breakfasts

A good hearty Scottish breakfast is the ideal way to start the morning, especially if your day involves energetic outdoor activities. Oats take many forms, from a warming dish of oatmeal porridge to a plate of oatcakes. Smoked fish, such as smoked haddock and salmon, is also popular, especially when made into a tasty kedgeree. The national favourite, black pudding, is a traditional breakfast staple, often served with eggs, bacon and Scottish morning rolls, a special breakfast bread enjoyed with jam or marmalade.

Left: Smoked fish, such as Arbroath smokies, eggs and home-made bread or bannocks, form the heart of the traditional Scottish breakfast.

porridge

One of Scotland's oldest foods, oatmeal porridge remains a favourite way to start the day, especially during winter or when you are about to go out for a day's walking on the hills. Brown sugar or honey, cream and a tot of whisky are treats added for weekend breakfasts. Serve with stewed plums for a low-fat breakfast.

1 Put the water, pinhead oatmeal and salt into a heavy pan and bring the mixture to the boil over a medium heat, stirring with a wooden spatula. When the porridge is smooth and beginning to thicken, reduce the heat to a simmer.

2 Cook over a gentle heat for about 25 minutes, stirring occasionally, until the oatmeal is cooked and the consistency smooth.

3 Serve hot with cold milk or cream and extra salt, if required.or with stewed plums and sugar or honey.

Variation
Modern rolled oats can be used, in the proportion of 115g/4oz/ generous 1 cup to 750ml/1¼ pints/3 cups water, plus a sprinkling of salt. This cooks more quickly than pinhead oatmeal. Simmer, stirring to prevent sticking, for about 5 minutes. Either type of oatmeal can be left to cook overnight in the slow oven of a range.

Serves 4

1 litre/1¾ pints/4 cups water
115g/4oz/1 cup pinhead oatmeal
good pinch of salt
stewed plums or single (light) cream
   with sugar or honey, to serve

Per portion Energy 115kcal/488kJ; Protein 3.6g; Carbohydrate 20.9g, of which sugars 0g; Fat 2.5g, of which saturates 0g; Cholesterol 0mg; Calcium 16mg; Fibre 2g; Sodium 304mg.

potato cakes

This is the traditional method of making potato cakes on a griddle or in a heavy frying pan. Commercial versions are available throughout Scotland as thin, pre-cooked potato cakes, which are fried to eat with a full breakfast of sausage, bacon and egg or to enjoy at high tea.

Makes about 12

675g/1½lb potatoes, peeled
25g/1oz/2 tbsp unsalted (sweet)
    butter
about 175g/6oz/1½ cups plain
    (all-purpose) flour
salt

1 Boil the potatoes in a large pan of water over a medium heat until tender, then drain thoroughly, replacing the pan with the drained potatoes over a low heat for a few minutes to allow any moisture to evaporate.

2 Mash the potatoes with salt to taste, then mix in the butter and cool.

3 Turn out on to a floured work surface and knead in about one-third of its volume in flour, or as much as is needed to make a pliable dough.

4 Roll out to a thickness of about 1cm/½in and cut into triangles.

5 Heat a dry griddle or heavy frying pan over a low heat and cook for about 3 minutes until browned.

6 Turn the potato cakes over and cook for a further 3 minutes until browned. Serve hot.

Per batch Energy 1276kcal/5392kJ; Protein 30.4g; Carbohydrate 249.1g, of which sugars 6.7g; Fat 24.1g, of which saturates 13.4g; Cholesterol 53mg; Calcium 282mg; Fibre 14g; Sodium 203mg.

Scottish morning rolls

These rolls are best served warm, as soon as they are baked. In Scotland they are a firm favourite for breakfast with a fried egg and bacon. They also go very well with a pat of fresh butter and homemade jams and jellies.

Makes 10

450g/1lb/4 cups unbleached plain (all-purpose) white flour, plus extra for dusting
10ml/2 tsp salt
20g/¾oz fresh yeast
150ml/¼ pint/⅔ cup lukewarm milk, plus extra for glazing
150ml/¼ pint/⅔ cup lukewarm water

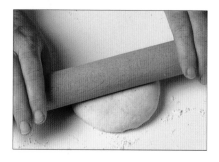

1 Grease two baking sheets. Sift the flour and salt together into a large bowl and make a well in the centre.

2 Mix the yeast with the milk, then mix in the water. Stir to dissolve. Add the yeast mixture to the centre of the flour and mix together to form a soft dough.

3 Knead the dough lightly then cover with lightly oiled clear film (plastic wrap) and leave to rise in a warm place for 1 hour, or until doubled in size. Turn the dough out on to a floured surface and knock back (punch down).

4 Divide the dough into 10 equal pieces. Knead each roll lightly and, using a rolling pin, shape each piece to a flat 10 x 7.5cm/4 x 3in oval or a flat 9cm/3½in round.

5 Transfer the rolls to the prepared baking sheets and cover with oiled clear film. Leave to rise in a warm place for about 30 minutes. Meanwhile, preheat the oven to 200°C/400°F/Gas 6.

6 Remove the clear film – the rolls should have risen slightly. Press each roll in the centre with your three middle fingers to equalize the air bubbles and to help prevent blistering.

7 Brush with milk and dust with flour. Bake for 15–20 minutes, or until lightly browned. As soon as you have taken the rolls out of the oven, dust with more flour and cool slightly on a wire rack. Serve warm.

Per roll Energy 160kcal/682kJ; Protein 4.7g; Carbohydrate 35.7g, of which sugars 1.4g; Fat 0.8g, of which saturates 0.3g; Cholesterol 1mg; Calcium 81mg; Fibre 1.4g; Sodium 401mg.

creamy scrambled eggs with smoked salmon

A special treat for weekend breakfasts, scrambled eggs served with locally produced smoked salmon is popular in some of Scotland's best guesthouses and hotels and makes a good alternative to the traditional fry-up.

Serves 1

3 eggs
15ml/1 tbsp single (light) cream
  or milk
knob (pat) of butter
1 slice of smoked salmon,
  chopped or whole, warmed
salt and ground black pepper
sprig of fresh parsley, to garnish
triangles of hot toast, to serve

Cook's Tip

For extra-creamy scrambled eggs, stir in a knob of butter when the eggs are nearly set and then add the cream at the last minute.

1 Whisk the eggs in a bowl together with half the cream or milk, a generous grinding of black pepper and a little salt to taste if you like, remembering that the smoked salmon may naturally be quite salty.

2 Melt the butter in a pan then add the egg mixture and stir until nearly set. Add the rest of the cream, which prevents the eggs from overcooking.

3 Either stir in the chopped smoked salmon or serve the warmed slice alongside the egg. Serve immediately on warmed plates.

Variation

For creamy scrambled eggs with bacon and cheese, first cook 1 or 2 rashers (strips) of streaky (fatty) bacon per person in a non-stick frying pan until crispy. Then chop the bacon, add it to the egg mixture and scramble over a gentle heat. Just before it sets, add 25g/1oz/¼ cup grated hard cheese, such as farmhouse Cheddar, and some freshly chopped herbs such as basil or chives. Mix together quickly and serve immediately on hot buttered toast.

Per portion Energy 447kcal/1862kJ; Protein 37.3g; Carbohydrate 0.4g, of which sugars 0.4g; Fat 33.6g, of which saturates 13.1g; Cholesterol 734mg; Calcium 128mg; Fibre 0g; Sodium 1.37g.

kedgeree

Of Indian origin, kedgeree came to Scotland via England and the landed gentry. It quickly became a popular meal using smoked fish for breakfast or high tea, and it even features on many contemporary restaurant menus. This is a more manageable dish than the full Scottish breakfast when feeding several people.

Serves 4–6

450g/1lb smoked haddock
300ml/½ pint/1¼ cups milk
175g/6oz/scant 1 cup long grain rice
pinch of grated nutmeg and
    cayenne pepper
50g/2oz/¼ cup butter
1 onion, peeled and finely chopped
2 hard-boiled eggs
salt and ground black pepper
chopped fresh parsley, to garnish
lemon wedges and wholemeal
    (whole-wheat) toast, to serve

Variation

Try using leftover cooked salmon, instead of the haddock.

1 Poach the haddock in the milk, made up with just enough water to cover the fish, for about 8 minutes, or until just cooked. Skin the haddock, remove all the bones and flake the flesh with a fork. Set aside.

2 Bring 600ml/1 pint/2½ cups water to the boil in a large pan. Add the rice, cover closely and cook over a low heat for about 25 minutes, or until all the water has been absorbed. Season with salt, pepper, nutmeg and cayenne.

3 Meanwhile, heat 15g/½oz/1 tbsp of the butter in a pan and fry the onion until soft and transparent. Set aside. Roughly chop one of the hard-boiled eggs, and slice the other into neat wedges.

4 Stir the remaining butter into the rice and add the flaked haddock, onion and the chopped egg. Season to taste and heat the mixture through gently (this can be done on a serving dish in a low oven if more convenient).

5 To serve, pile the kedgeree on a warmed dish, sprinkle with parsley and arrange the wedges of egg and lemon on top. Serve hot with the toast.

Per portion Energy 399kcal/1668kJ; Protein 28.9g; Carbohydrate 38g, of which sugars 2.2g; Fat 14.6g, of which saturates 7.6g; Cholesterol 181mg; Calcium 62mg; Fibre 0.5g; Sodium 974mg.

Lorn sausage

The Firth of Lorn, the region from which this dish originated, cuts through Argyll between the island of Mull and the west coast of Scotland. Prepared traditionally in a loaf shape and chilled overnight, the sausage is then sliced before cooking. Accompanied with a spicy red onion relish, it makes a delicious meal.

Serves 4

900g/2lb minced (ground) beef
65g/2½oz/generous 1 cup stale
    white breadcrumbs
150g/5oz/scant 1 cup semolina
5ml/1 tsp salt
75ml/5 tbsp water
ground black pepper
grilled (broiled) tomatoes and red
    onion relish, to serve

Cook's Tip

For the best results, use standard minced (ground) beef when making Lorn sausage rather than lean minced steak, as the higher fat content helps bind the ingredients together.

1 In a large mixing bowl, combine the beef, breadcrumbs, semolina and salt together thoroughly with a fork.

2 Pour in the water, mix again and season to taste. Pass the beef mixture through a coarse mincer (grinder) and set aside.

3 Carefully line a 1.3kg/3lb loaf tin (pan) with clear film (plastic wrap).

4 Spoon the sausage mixture into the tin, pressing it in firmly with the back of a wooden spoon. Even out the surface of the sausage mixture and fold the clear film over the top. Chill overnight or for 2–3 hours.

5 When ready to cook, preheat the grill (broiler). Turn the sausage out of the tin on to a chopping board and cut into 1cm/½in slices. Grill (broil) each slice for about 8–10 minutes until cooked through, turning once. Alternatively, fry for about 8–10 minutes until cooked through, again turning once.

6 Serve with grilled (broiled) tomatoes and red onion relish.

Per portion Energy 691kcal/2886kJ; Protein 50.1g; Carbohydrate 40.7g, of which sugars 0.4g; Fat 37.4g, of which saturates 15.6g; Cholesterol 135mg; Calcium 47mg; Fibre 1.1g; Sodium 299mg.

soups and appetizers

Scotland's extensive coastline, lochs and rivers means that its first courses and soups are often based on smoked and fresh fish and shellfish, from the simple raw oyster to Cullen Skink and Hot Crab Soufflés. The sensational smoked salmons that are now being produced provide a sumptuous start to any meal, simply sprinkled with ground black pepper and a squeeze of fresh lemon. Other smoked products, game and wonderful cheeses also make delicious first courses.

Left: Potatoes, onions and fish form the heart of many satisfying home-made soups including the world-famous Cullen Skink.

leek and potato soup

This is a hearty Scottish staple, forming everything from a warming winter lunch to a hot drink from a flask by the loch on a cold afternoon. The chopped leeks, onion and potato produce a chunky soup. If you prefer your soup to have a smooth texture, strain the mixure instead of processing.

Serves 4

50g/2oz/¼ cup butter
2 leeks, washed and chopped
1 small onion, peeled and finely
  chopped
350g/12oz potatoes, peeled
  and chopped
900ml/1½ pints/3¾ cups chicken
  or vegetable stock
salt and ground black pepper
chopped fresh parsley, to garnish

Variation

Stir in 120ml/4fl oz/½ cup single (light) cream when you add the remaining butter for a deliciously creamy soup.

1 Heat 25g/1oz/2 tbsp of the butter in a large pan over a medium heat. Add the leeks and onion and cook gently, stirring occasionally, for about 7 minutes, until they are softened but not browned.

2 Add the potatoes to the pan and cook for about 2–3 minutes, then add the stock and bring to the boil. Cover and simmer for 30–35 minutes.

3 Season to taste and remove the pan from the heat. Dice and stir in the remaining butter. Garnish with the chopped parsley and serve hot.

Cook's Tips

• Don't use a food processor to purée this soup as it can give the potatoes a gluey consistency. The potatoes should be left to crumble and disintegrate naturally as they boil, making the consistency of the soup thicker the longer you leave them.
• Add nutritional value to your soup by making your own chicken or vegetable stock. Simmer bones and vegetables, including carrots, onions and leeks, in water for 2 hours, skim off any fat and strain the liquid before use.

Per portion Energy 179kcal/747kJ; Protein 3.2g; Carbohydrate 17.9g, of which sugars 4g; Fat 11g, of which saturates 6.7g; Cholesterol 27mg; Calcium 32mg; Fibre 3g; Sodium 88mg.

Cullen skink

The famous Cullen skink comes from the fishing port of Cullen on the east coast of Scotland, the word "skink" meaning an essence or soup. The fishermen smoked their smaller fish and these, with locally grown potatoes, formed their staple diet.

3 Strain the fish stock and return to the pan, then add the potatoes and simmer for about 25 minutes, or until tender.

4 Carefully remove the potatoes from the pan using a slotted spoon. Add the milk to the pan and bring to the boil.

5 In a separate pan, mash the potatoes with the butter. A little at a time, whisk the potato mixture thoroughly into the pan until the soup is thick and creamy.

6 Add the flaked fish to the pan and adjust the seasoning. Sprinkle with chives and serve immediately with fresh crusty bread.

Serves 6

1 Finnan haddock or other smoked
  haddock, about 350g/12oz
1 onion, chopped
bouquet garni
900ml/1½ pints/3¾ cups water
500g/1¼ lb potatoes, quartered
600ml/1 pint/2½ cups milk
40g/1½oz/3 tbsp butter
salt and ground black pepper
chopped chives, to garnish

1 Put the haddock, onion, bouquet garni and water into a large pan and bring to the boil. Skim with a slotted spoon, then cover the pan. Reduce the heat and gently poach for 10–15 minutes, until the fish flakes easily.

2 Lift the fish from the pan and remove the skin and any bones. Return the skin and bones to the pan and simmer, uncovered, for a further 30 minutes. Flake the cooked fish flesh.

Per portion Energy 205kcal/864kJ; Protein 16.1g; Carbohydrate 19g, of which sugars 6.4g; Fat 7.8g, of which saturates 4.7g; Cholesterol 41mg; Calcium 137mg; Fibre 1g; Sodium 132mg.

Scotch broth

Sustaining and warming, Scotch broth is custom-made for chilly Scottish weather, and makes a delicious winter soup anywhere. Traditionally, a large pot of it is made and this is dipped into over the next few days, the flavour improving all the time.

Serves 6–8

1kg/2¼lb lean neck (US shoulder or breast) of lamb, cut into large, even-sized chunks
1.75 litres/3 pints/7½ cups cold water
1 large onion, chopped
50g/2oz/¼ cup pearl barley
bouquet garni
1 large carrot, chopped
1 turnip, chopped
3 leeks, chopped
1 small white cabbage, finely shredded
salt and ground black pepper
chopped fresh parsley, to garnish

1 Put the lamb and water in a large pan over a medium heat and gently bring to the boil. Skim off the scum with a slotted spoon. Add the onion, pearl barley and bouquet garni, and stir in thoroughly.

2 Bring the soup back to the boil, then reduce the heat, partly cover the pan and simmer gently for a further 1 hour. Make sure that it does not boil too rapidly or go dry.

3 Add the remaining vegetables to the pan and season with salt and ground black pepper. Bring to the boil, partly cover again and simmer for about 35 minutes, until the vegetables are tender.

4 Remove the surplus fat from the top of the soup with a sheet of kitchen paper. Serve the soup hot, garnished with chopped parsley, with chunks of fresh bread.

Per portion Energy 387kcal/1619kJ; Protein 36.2g; Carbohydrate 17.7g, of which sugars 9.1g; Fat 19.5g, of which saturates 8.8g; Cholesterol 127mg; Calcium 86mg; Fibre 4.3g; Sodium 157mg.

grilled oysters with Highland heather honey

Scottish heather honey has an especially fragrant scent. The pollen is gathered by bees late in the season when the heather on the moors is in full flower. Beekeepers in Scotland will take their hives up to the hills once the spring and early summer blossoms are over, so that the flavour becomes even more intense.

Serves 4

1 bunch spring onions (scallions),
  washed
20ml/4 tsp heather honey
10ml/2 tsp soy sauce
16 fresh oysters

1 Preheat the grill (broiler) to medium. Chop the spring onions finely, removing any coarser outer leaves.

2 Place the heather honey and soy sauce in a bowl and mix. Then add the finely chopped spring onions and mix them in thoroughly.

3 Discard any oysters that are already open. Then open the oysters with an oyster knife or a small, sharp knife, catching the liquid in a small bowl. Discard the liquid and broken shell. Leave the oysters attached to one side of the shell.

4 Place a large teaspoon of the honey and spring onion mixture on top of each of the prepared oysters.

5 Place under the preheated grill until the mixture bubbles, which will take about 5 minutes. Take care when removing the oysters from the grill as the shells retain the heat. Make sure that you don't lose any of the sauce from inside the oyster shells.

6 Allow the oysters to cool slightly before serving with slices of fresh white bread to soak up the juices. Either tip them straight into your mouth or lift them out with a spoon or fork.

Cook's Tip

Once plentiful, oysters are now a delicacy and are usually eaten raw. Buy them with their shells tightly clamped together, showing that they are still alive.

Per portion Energy 81kcal/343kJ; Protein 9.2g; Carbohydrate 9.1g, of which sugars 6.9g; Fat 1.2g, of which saturates 0.2g; Cholesterol 46mg; Calcium 121mg; Fibre 0.3g; Sodium 588mg.

smoked haddock pâté

Arbroath smokies are small haddock that are beheaded and gutted but not split before being dry-salted and hot-smoked to a rich copper colour, leaving the insides creamy white. They are still made in family-run smokehouses around Arbroath.

Serves 6

3 Arbroath smokies, 225g/8oz each
275g/10oz/1¼ cups soft cheese
3 eggs, beaten
30–45ml/2–3 tbsp lemon juice
ground black pepper
butter for greasing
sprigs of chervil, to garnish
lettuce and lemon wedges, to serve

1 Preheat the oven to 160°C/325°F/Gas 3. Butter six ramekin dishes.

2 Lay the smokies in a baking dish and heat through in the oven for 10 minutes.

3 Remove the fish from the oven, carefully remove the skin and bones then flake the flesh into a bowl.

4 Mash the fish with a fork then work in the cheese, then the eggs. Add lemon juice and pepper to taste.

5 Divide the fish mixture among the ramekin dishes and place them in a large roasting pan. Pour hot water into the roasting pan to come halfway up the dishes.

6 Bake the ramekin dishes in the oven for 30 minutes, until the fish mixture is just set.

7 Leave the ramekins to cool for 2–3 minutes, then run a sharp knife around the edge of each dish and carefully invert the pâté on to warmed plates.

8 Garnish the pâté with chervil sprigs and serve with the lettuce leaves and lemon wedges.

Variation

Kippers or any other smoked fish, including salmon, mackerel or trout, can be used in this recipe.

Per portion Energy 206kcal/859kJ; Protein 25.3g; Carbohydrate 1.7g, of which sugars 0.1g; Fat 11g, of which saturates 5.8g; Cholesterol 153mg; Calcium 82mg; Fibre 0g; Sodium 940mg.

hot crab soufflés

These delicious little soufflés must be served as soon as they are ready, so seat your guests at the table before taking the soufflés out of the oven. Use local, freshly caught crabs if possible, although canned or frozen will do if necessary.

Serves 6

50g/2oz/¼ cup butter, plus extra
   for greasing
45ml/3 tbsp fine wholemeal (whole-
   wheat) breadcrumbs
4 spring onions (scallions), chopped
15ml/1 tbsp Malaysian or mild
   Madras curry powder
25g/1oz/¼ cup plain (all-purpose)
   flour
105ml/7 tbsp coconut milk or milk
150ml/¼ pint/⅔ cup whipping
   cream
4 eggs, separated, plus 2 egg whites
225g/8oz white crab meat
mild green Tabasco sauce, to taste
salt and ground black pepper

1 Use a little of the butter to grease six ramekins. Sprinkle in the breadcrumbs to coat and tip out any excess crumbs. Preheat the oven to 200°C/400°F/Gas 6.

2 Melt the remaining butter in a pan, add the spring onions and curry powder and cook for 1 minute. Stir in the flour and cook for 1 minute more.

3 Gradually add the coconut milk or milk and cream, stirring continuously. Cook, stirring, over a low heat until smooth and thick.

4 Off the heat, stir in the egg yolks, then the crab meat. Season with salt, black pepper and Tabasco sauce.

5 Beat the egg whites stiffly with a pinch of salt. Stir one-third into the crab mixture to lighten it; fold in the rest. Spoon into the ramekins.

6 Bake for 8 minutes until well risen and golden brown, and firm to the touch. Serve immediately.

Per portion Energy 234kcal/972kJ; Protein 11.8g; Carbohydrate 8.7g, of which sugars 1.8g; Fat 17.1g, of which saturates 9.3g; Cholesterol 97mg; Calcium 37mg; Fibre 0.3g; Sodium 322mg.

strawberry and smoked venison salad

The combination of strawberries, balsamic vinegar and smoked venison creates a perfect ménage à trois. The tang of the vinegar sets off the sweetness of the strawberries, and adds a fruity contrast to the rich, dry, smoky venison.

Serves 4

12 ripe Scottish strawberries
2.5ml/½ tsp caster (superfine) sugar
5ml/1 tsp balsamic vinegar
8 thin slices of smoked venison
mixed salad leaves

For the dressing
10ml/2 tsp olive oil
5ml/1 tsp balsamic vinegar
splash of strawberry wine (optional)
salt and ground black pepper

Variation
Replace the smoked venison with smoked chicken or pheasant.

1 Slice the strawberries vertically into three or four pieces then place in a bowl with the sugar and balsamic vinegar. Leave for 30 minutes.

2 Meanwhile, make the dressing by placing the olive oil and balsamic vinegar in a small bowl and whisking them together with the wine, if you are using it. Add salt and ground black pepper to taste.

3 Cut the smoked venison into little strips. Put the salad leaves in a bowl and toss with the dressing. Distribute the salad leaves among four plates, sprinkle with the strawberries and venison and serve immediately.

Cook's Tips
• Suitable salad leaves include lollo rosso for colour, rocket (arugula) for a peppery flavour and Little Gem (Bibb) for crunch.
• The sugar brings out the moisture in the strawberries, which combines with the balsamic vinegar to create a lovely shiny coating. Do not leave them to stand for too long as they can become tired looking – 30 minutes is about right.

Per portion Energy 116kcal/486kJ; Protein 11.6g; Carbohydrate 3.1g, of which sugars 3.1g; Fat 6.8g, of which saturates 1.2g; Cholesterol 25mg; Calcium 16mg; Fibre 0.6g; Sodium 31mg.

main courses

Central to the Scottish way of life, fish from the sea, loch and river, game from the hills and poultry from the crofts have always proved a mainstay of the national cuisine. Wild salmon is the king of Scottish fish, but fishing villages in the Highlands and Islands still bring in a daily catch of haddock, sea trout, lobsters, crabs and prawns. Scottish beef is renowned all over the world because it is reared in a natural environment. Traditionally venison was wild, but today it is farmed like lamb and pork, producing succulent meat that is widely available for making some wonderful dishes.

Left: Fresh wild salmon has deep pink flesh with a superb flavour and forms the basis of many classic Scottish main courses.

clam stovies

Clams are now harvested in the lochs, especially in Loch Fyne where some of the best Scottish clams are grown on ropes. Limpets or cockles can also be used if you can buy them fresh or collect them yourself along the seashore.

Serves 4

2.5 litres/4 pints/10 cups clams
potatoes (see step 3)
oil, for greasing
chopped fresh flat leaf parsley, to
  garnish
50g/2oz/¼ cup butter
salt and ground black pepper

1 Wash the clams and soak them overnight in fresh cold water. This will clean them out and get rid of any sand and other detritus.

2 Preheat the oven to 190°C/375°F/Gas 5. Put the clams into a large pan, cover with water and bring to the boil. Add a little salt then simmer until the shells open. Reserve the cooking liquor. Shell the clams, discarding any that failed to open, reserving a few whole.

3 Weigh the shelled clams. You will need three times their weight in potatoes.

4 Peel and slice the potatoes thinly. Lightly oil the base and sides of a flameproof, ovenproof dish. Arrange a layer of potatoes in the base of the dish, add a layer of the clams and season with a little salt and ground black pepper. Repeat until the ingredients are all used, finishing with a layer of potatoes on top. Finally, season lightly.

5 Pour in some of the reserved cooking liquor to come about halfway up the dish. Dot the top with the butter then cover with foil. Bring to the boil on the stove over a medium-high heat, then bake in the preheated oven for 2 hours until the top is golden brown.

6 Serve hot, garnished with chopped fresh flat leaf parsley.

Variation

To make cockle and mussel stovies, replace the clams with 175g/6oz shelled cooked mussels and 115g/4oz shelled cooked cockles; include any liquor left from cooking the mussels and cockles. Reserve a few cockles and mussels in their shells for garnish, if you like.

Per portion Energy 320kcal/1348kJ; Protein 17.3g; Carbohydrate 36.7g, of which sugars 3.3g; Fat 12.6g, of which saturates 7g; Cholesterol 57mg; Calcium 188mg; Fibre 2.9g; Sodium 262mg.

flaky smoked salmon with potatoes

Salar is a type of smoked salmon with a characteristic flavour, made on the island of South Uist in the Outer Hebrides, although other smoked fish can be used in this recipe.

1 Cook the potatoes until just done, then drain and leave to cool until you can handle them.

2 Meanwhile, for the dressing, mix the balsamic vinegar and olive oil together. Toss the mixed salad leaves in the dressing then divide between four individual serving plates.

3 Cut the potatoes in two and mix with a little olive oil. The warmth of the potatoes will create a great smell and bring out the flavour.

4 Arrange the potatoes over the salad leaves and place the smoked salmon on top. Garnish with a few torn fresh basil leaves and serve with crusty bread.

Serves 4

12 small new potatoes
4 x Salar flaky salmon steaks, about
 75g/3oz each
mixed salad leaves
a little olive oil
a few fresh basil leaves, to garnish

For the dressing

10ml/2 tsp balsamic vinegar
20ml/4 tsp virgin olive oil

Cook's Tips

• Choose small, tasty new potatoes, such as baby Maris Piper or King Edwards. Make sure that they are not overcooked as they need to retain some firmness.
• Almost any fresh white or hot-smoked fish is suitable for this dish; smoked cod and haddock are particularly good. A mixture of smoked and unsmoked fish also works well.

Per portion Energy 322kcal/1342kJ; Protein 17.3g; Carbohydrate 20.1g, of which sugars 1.6g; Fat 19.6g, of which saturates 3.1g; Cholesterol 38mg; Calcium 23mg; Fibre 1.3g; Sodium 48mg.

salmon fishcakes

The secret of a good fishcake is to make it with freshly prepared fish and potatoes, homemade breadcrumbs and plenty of interesting seasoning.

Serves 4

450g/1lb cooked salmon fillet
450g/1lb freshly cooked potatoes, mashed
25g/1oz/2 tbsp butter, melted
10ml/2 tsp wholegrain mustard
15ml/1 tbsp each chopped fresh dill and chopped fresh flat leaf parsley
grated rind and juice of ½ lemon
15g/½oz/1 tbsp plain (all-purpose) flour
1 egg, lightly beaten
150g/5oz/generous 1 cup dried breadcrumbs
60ml/4 tbsp sunflower oil
salt and ground white pepper
rocket (arugula) leaves and fresh chives, to garnish
lemon wedges, to serve

1 Flake the cooked salmon, discarding any skin and bones. Mix the salmon in a bowl with the potato, butter and mustard. Stir in the dill and parsley, lemon rind and juice. Season well.

2 Divide the mixture into eight thick discs. Dip the fishcakes first in flour, then in egg and finally in breadcrumbs, making sure they are evenly coated.

3 Heat the oil in a frying pan until very hot. Fry the fishcakes in batches until golden brown and crisp all over. Drain on kitchen paper and keep hot.

4 Warm four plates and then place two fishcakes on to each plate, one slightly on top of the other. Garnish with rocket leaves and chives, and serve with lemon wedges.

Per portion Energy 586kcal/2453kJ; Protein 29.8g; Carbohydrate 49.9g, of which sugars 3.2g; Fat 31g, of which saturates 7.2g; Cholesterol 117mg; Calcium 79mg; Fibre 1.3g; Sodium 266mg.

stoved chicken

The word "stoved" is derived not from the word stove but from the French *étuver* – to cook in a covered pot – and originates from the time of the Franco/Scottish Alliance in the 17th century. Instead of using chicken joints, this recipe also works well with either chicken thighs or chicken drumsticks.

Serves 4

900g/2lb potatoes, cut into
   5mm/¼in slices
2 large onions, thinly sliced
15ml/1 tbsp chopped fresh thyme
25g/1oz/¼ stick butter
15ml/1 tbsp vegetable oil
2 large bacon rashers (strips),
   chopped
4 large chicken joints, halved
1 bay leaf
600ml/1 pint/2½ cups chicken stock
salt and ground black pepper

Variation

Use chopped fresh French tarragon instead of the thyme.

1 Preheat the oven to 150°C/300°F/Gas 2. Make a thick layer of half the potato slices in the base of a large, heavy casserole, then cover with half the onion. Sprinkle with half the thyme and salt and ground black pepper.

2 Heat the butter and oil in a large frying pan then brown the bacon and chicken. Using a slotted spoon, transfer the chicken and bacon to the casserole. Reserve the fat in the pan.

3 Tuck the bay leaf in between the chicken. Sprinkle the remaining thyme over, then cover with the remaining onion, followed by a neat layer of overlapping potato slices. Season.

4 Pour the stock into the casserole. Brush the top layer of the sliced potatoes with the reserved fat, then cover tightly and cook in the preheated oven for about 2 hours, until the chicken is thoroughly cooked and tender.

5 Preheat the grill (broiler) to high. Uncover the casserole and place under the grill and cook until the potato slices begin to brown and crisp. Serve hot.

Per portion Energy 630kcal/2653kJ; Protein 69.2g; Carbohydrate 48.2g, of which sugars 8.9g; Fat 19.2g, of which saturates 7.2g; Cholesterol 195mg; Calcium 57mg; Fibre 3.9g; Sodium 574mg.

pan-fried pheasant with oatmeal and cream sauce

Rolled oats are often used for coating fish before pan-frying, but this treatment is equally good with tender poultry, game and other meats. Sweet, slightly tangy redcurrant jelly is used to bind the oatmeal to the tender pheasant breast fillets.

Serves 4

115g/4oz/generous 1 cup medium
   rolled oats
4 skinless, boneless pheasant
   breasts
45ml/3 tbsp redcurrant jelly, melted
50g/2oz/¼ cup butter
15ml/1 tbsp olive oil
45ml/3 tbsp wholegrain mustard
300ml/½ pint/1¼ cups double
   (heavy) cream
salt and ground black pepper

Variation
Replace the pheasant with skinless, boneless chicken breasts.

1 Place the rolled oats on a plate and season well with salt and ground black pepper.

2 Brush the skinned boneless pheasant breasts with the melted redcurrant jelly, then turn them in the rolled oats to coat them evenly. Shake off any excess oats and set them to one side.

3 Heat the butter and oil in a frying pan until foaming. Add the pheasant breasts and cook over a high heat, turning frequently, until they are golden brown on all sides.

4 Reduce the heat to medium and cook for a further 8–10 minutes, turning once or twice, until the meat is thoroughly cooked.

5 Add the mustard and cream, stirring to combine with the cooking juices. Bring slowly to the boil then simmer for 10 minutes over a low heat, or until the sauce has thickened to a good consistency. Serve immediately.

Per portion Energy 847kcal/3520kJ; Protein 37.1g; Carbohydrate 30.1g, of which sugars 9.1g; Fat 59g, of which saturates 35.1g; Cholesterol 129mg; Calcium 105mg; Fibre 2g; Sodium 205mg.

haggis with clapshot cake

Haggis is probably the best known of all Scottish traditional dishes, not least because of the famous Burns poem, "Ode to a Haggis" which is recited in front of a haggis at suppers on Burns Night. This is the traditional haggis recipe served with turnip and potato clapshot – a variation on "haggis with neeps and tatties".

Serves 4

1 large haggis, approximately
   800g/1¾lb
450g/1lb peeled turnip or swede
   (rutabaga), cut into 5mm/¼in
   slices
225g/8oz peeled potatoes, cut
   into 5mm/¼in slices
120ml/4fl oz/½ cup milk
1 garlic clove, crushed with
   5ml/1 tsp salt
175ml/6fl oz/¾ cup double
   (heavy) cream
freshly grated nutmeg
ground black pepper
butter, for greasing

1 Preheat the oven to 180°C/350°F/Gas 4. Wrap the haggis in foil, covering it completely and folding over the edges of the foil. Place the haggis in a roasting pan with about 2.5cm/1in water. Heat in the oven for 30–40 minutes.

2 Put the sliced vegetables in a large pan and add the milk and salted garlic. Stir over a low heat until the potatoes break down and the liquid thickens.

3 Stir in the cream, nutmeg and black pepper. Slowly bring to the boil, reduce the heat and simmer gently for a few minutes.

4 Butter a deep round 18cm/7in ovenproof dish or a small roasting pan. Transfer the vegetable mixture to the dish or pan. Bake in the oven for about 1 hour. If the top is becoming too brown, cover it with foil and continue baking.

5 Remove the foil from the haggis, place on a warmed serving dish and bring out to the table for your guests to witness the cutting. Use a sharp knife to cut through the skin then spoon out the haggis on to warmed plates. Serve the clapshot cake in slices with the haggis, spooning any juices over.

Per portion Energy 918kcal/3819kJ; Protein 24.9g; Carbohydrate 55.3g, of which sugars 8.5g; Fat 67.9g, of which saturates 30.2g; Cholesterol 244mg; Calcium 180mg; Fibre 3.1g; Sodium 1586mg.

griddled loin of lamb with barley risotto

Scottish lamb and mutton is renowned for its flavour and quality. A loin of lamb is taken from the back or the saddle, and it should be completely clear of fat or gristle so you are getting pure meat. Barley is a popular grain throughout Scotland, and when used in a risotto makes for a deliciously flavourful dish.

Serves 4

a little olive oil
750ml/1¼ pints/3 cups chicken
    stock
75g/3oz/6 tbsp butter
1 onion, finely chopped
225g/8oz/1 cup barley
50g/2oz Bonnet cheese
3 loins of lamb
salt and ground black pepper
virgin olive oil, to serve

Cook's Tip

You may need less or more liquid depending on the barley.

1 Melt the butter and sweat the onion. Bring the stock to the boil.

2 Add the barley and stir well. Add one-third of the stock. Bring to the boil then reduce the heat, stirring all the time until the liquid is absorbed. Add half of the remaining stock and stir. Finally stir in the rest of the stock.

3 Grate the cheese and add to the barley when it has absorbed all the stock. Stir in well, season with salt and ground black pepper, and keep warm.

4 Prepare a cast-iron ridged griddle or heavy pan by brushing it with olive oil. Heat the griddle or heavy pan until very hot. Brush the lamb with olive oil and season well. Sear the lamb quickly all over, then reduce the heat and cook for a further 8 minutes, turning occasionally. Leave in a warm place to rest for 5 minutes.

5 Carve four thickish slices from each loin. Add a splash of virgin olive oil to the risotto, place a mound of risotto on each plate and prop the slices of lamb on it.

Per portion Energy 827kcal/3460kJ; Protein 49.8g; Carbohydrate 53.2g, of which sugars 2.2g; Fat 47.7g, of which saturates 25.2g; Cholesterol 223mg; Calcium 55mg; Fibre 0.5g; Sodium 348mg.

beef stew with oysters and beer

Oysters were once very cheap, sold by "oyster lassies" in Edinburgh, calling their familiar cry, "Wha'll o' caller ou?" – "Who will have fresh oysters?"

Serves 4

1kg/2¼lb rump (round) steak
6 thin rashers (strips) bacon
12 oysters
25g/1oz/¼ cup plain (all-purpose) flour
generous pinch of cayenne pepper
butter or olive oil, for greasing
3 shallots, finely chopped
300ml/½ pint/1¼ cups beer
salt and ground black pepper

1 Preheat the oven to 180°C/350°F/Gas 4. Place the steaks one at a time between sheets of clear film (plastic wrap) and beat it with a rolling pin until it is flattened and thin. Slice the meat into 24 thin strips, wide enough to roll around an oyster.

2 Stretch the bacon rashers lengthways by placing them on a chopping board and, holding one end down with your thumb, pulling them out using the thick side of a sharp knife. Cut each rasher into four pieces.

3 Discard any oysters that are already open. Then open the oysters with an oyster knife or a small, sharp knife, catching the liquid in a small bowl. Discard the liquid and any broken shell. Cut each oyster in half lengthways and roll each piece in a strip of bacon. Then roll in a strip of beef so no oyster is visible.

4 Season the flour to taste with the cayenne pepper and salt and black pepper, then roll the meat in it.

5 Lightly grease a large flameproof casserole with butter or olive oil. Sprinkle the shallots over the base. Place the floured meat rolls on top, evenly spaced.

6 Slowly pour over the beer, bring to the boil, then cover and cook in the oven for 1½–2 hours until completely tender.

7 The flour will have thickened the stew sauce and produced a lovely, rich gravy. Serve with creamy mashed potatoes and fresh steamed vegetables.

Cook's Tip

To open the oysters use an oyster knife, grasping the oyster in your other hand with a dish towel. If you don't have an oyster knife, use a small knife or a pen knife, but be careful not to cut yourself as the blade can easily slip.

Per portion Energy 528kcal/2208kJ; Protein 61.4g; Carbohydrate 12.7g, of which sugars 2.5g; Fat 24.4g, of which saturates 10.1g; Cholesterol 182mg; Calcium 52mg; Fibre 0.6g; Sodium 634mg.

side dishes

As tasty and traditional as the main course itself, the vegetables and salads in Scottish cuisine will provide a healthy or hearty accompaniment to every meal. The richly flavoured green vegetables, including kale, chard, spinach and cabbage, are excellent served on their own or with a sauce.

A dish of oatmeal skirlie or a plate of potato-and-cabbage kailkenny will form an excellent accompaniment to roast meat. No meal is complete, however, without those robust root vegetables: turnip, swede, parsnip, carrot and the versatile favourite, the potato.

Left: Vegetables form an integral part of the Scottish diet from boiled potatoes and kale with mustard dressing to braised red cabbage.

kale with mustard dressing

Traditionally, sea kale is used for this dish. Its pale green fronds have a slightly nutty taste. Use curly kale if you can't get sea kale, although you will need to boil it for a few minutes before chilling and serving.

2 If you are using curly kale, wash it carefully to remove any grit and drain it thoroughly. Then place it in a large pan and bring to the boil for a few minutes. Drain and refresh in cold water.

3 Whisk the oil into the mustard in a bowl. When it is blended completely, whisk in the white wine vinegar. It should begin to thicken.

4 Season the mustard dressing to taste with sugar, salt and ground black pepper.

5 Toss the kale in the mustard dressing until it is thoroughly coated and serve immediately.

Serves 4

250g/9oz sea kale or curly kale
45ml/3 tbsp light olive oil
5ml/1 tsp wholegrain mustard
15ml/1 tbsp white wine vinegar
pinch of caster (superfine) sugar
salt and ground black pepper

1 If you are using sea kale, wash and drain it thoroughly, then trim it. Cut it into two along the line of the stem.

Variation

This recipe also works well with any leafy dark green vegetables such as Savoy cabbage or spinach.

Per portion Energy 99kcal/409kJ; Protein 2.1g; Carbohydrate 1.9g, of which sugars 1.9g; Fat 9.3g, of which saturates 1.3g; Cholesterol 0mg; Calcium 82mg; Fibre 2g; Sodium 27mg.

braised red cabbage

Red cabbage is a hardy vegetable that can be grown in a garden plot even in the difficult conditions of the Highlands and Islands. Lightly spiced with a sharp, sweet flavour, braised red cabbage goes well with roast pork, duck and game dishes.

Serves 4–6

1kg/2¼lb red cabbage
2 cooking apples
2 onions, chopped
5ml/1 tsp freshly grated nutmeg
1.5ml/¼ tsp ground cloves
1.5ml/¼ tsp ground cinnamon
15ml/1 tbsp soft dark brown sugar
45ml/3 tbsp red wine vinegar
25g/1oz/2 tbsp butter, diced
salt and ground black pepper
chopped flat leaf parsley, to garnish

1 Preheat the oven to 160°C/325°F/ Gas 3. Cut away and discard the large white ribs from the outer cabbage leaves using a large, sharp knife, then finely shred the cabbage.

2 Peel, core and coarsely grate the cooking apples.

3 Layer the shredded cabbage in a large ovenproof dish with the onions, apples, spices, sugar, and salt and ground black pepper. Pour over the vinegar and add the diced butter.

4 Cover the dish with a lid and cook in the preheated oven for about 1½ hours, stirring a couple of times, until the cabbage is very tender.

5 Serve the braised cabbage immediately, garnished with the chopped parsley.

Per portion Energy 160kcal/668kJ; Protein 4.3g; Carbohydrate 23.8g, of which sugars 22.4g; Fat 5.8g, of which saturates 3.3g; Cholesterol 13mg; Calcium 140mg; Fibre 6.6g; Sodium 58mg.

skirlie

Oatmeal has been a staple in Scotland for centuries. Skirlie is a simple preparation that can be used for stuffings or as an accompaniment, and is especially good with roast meats. It is traditionally cooked in lard but many people prefer butter.

2 Stir in the rolled oats and season well with salt and freshly ground black pepper. Cook gently for 10 minutes. Taste for seasoning and serve immediately.

Cook's Tip

Skirlie made with butter makes an excellent stuffing for roast chicken, pheasant or guinea-fowl.

Serves 4

50g/2oz/¼ cup butter
1 onion, finely chopped
175g/6oz/scant 2 cups medium
    rolled oats
salt and ground black pepper

Variation

To add a lovely rich flavour to the skirlie, grate in a little ground nutmeg cinnamon just before serving.

1 Melt the butter in a pan over a medium heat and add the onion. Fry gently until soft and slightly browned.

Per portion Energy 282kcal/1182kJ; Protein 6g; Carbohydrate 34.9g, of which sugars 2.2g; Fat 14.2g, of which saturates 6.5g; Cholesterol 27mg; Calcium 36mg; Fibre 3.5g; Sodium 91mg.

kailkenny

This is a mashed potato combination dish, originating from north-east Scotland. Normally the cabbage is boiled but it is more nutritious to quickly fry it, keeping in the goodness. Kailkenny makes an excellent accompaniment to any meat dish.

Serves 4

450g/1lb potatoes, peeled
50g/2oz/¼ cup butter
50ml/2fl oz/¼ cup milk
450g/1lb cabbage, finely shredded
30ml/2 tbsp olive oil
50ml/2fl oz/¼ cup double
    (heavy) cream
salt and ground black pepper

1 Cut the potatoes into small pieces, place in boiling water and boil for 15–20 minutes. Drain, replace on the heat for a few minutes then mash.

2 Heat the butter and milk in a small pan and then mix into the mashed potatoes. Season to taste.

3 Heat the olive oil in a large frying pan, add the shredded cabbage and fry for a few minutes. Season to taste with salt and ground black pepper.

4 Add the mashed potato, mix well then stir in the cream. Serve immediately.

Per portion Energy 183kcal/766kJ; Protein 3.9g; Carbohydrate 24g, of which sugars 7.3g; Fat 8.5g, of which saturates 2.4g; Cholesterol 7mg; Calcium 73mg; Fibre 3.5g; Sodium 24mg.

desserts and baking

The Scots are well known for their sweet tooth, and there are plenty of delicious traditional desserts, cakes and bakes to choose from. A recurring theme is fresh berries – especially raspberries – baked in tarts, crumbles and pies or blended with creams and other dairy products. The creams and yogurts are a speciality of the Lowlands, although throughout much of Scotland many households would have made their own. Dried fruit and nuts are favourite ingredients for cakes, including the famous Dundee cake with almonds baked decoratively around the top.

Left: Scottish desserts and bakes are rich in fruits and berries from the kitchen garden and eggs, butter and cream from the dairy.

cranachan

This lovely, nutritious dish is based on a traditional Scottish recipe originally made to celebrate the Harvest Festival. It can be enjoyed, as the original recipe was, as a teatime treat or a dessert, but it is also excellent served for breakfast or brunch. Try fresh blueberries or blackberries in place of the raspberries, too.

Serves 4

75g/3oz crunchy oat cereal
600ml/1 pint/2½ cups Greek (US strained plain) yogurt
250g/9oz/1⅓ cups raspberries
heather honey, to serve

Variations
• You can use almost any berries for this recipe. Strawberries and blackberries work very well. If you use strawberries, remove the stalks and cut them into quarters beforehand.
• If you feel especially decadent, you can use clotted cream instead of yogurt.

1 Preheat the grill (broiler) to high.

2 Spread the oat cereal on a baking sheet and place under the hot grill for 3–4 minutes, stirring regularly.

3 Break up any lumps in the oat cereal with a metal spoon. Set the oatmeal aside on a plate to cool. When the cereal has cooled completely, fold it into the Greek yogurt.

4 Gently fold 200g/7oz/generous 1 cup of the raspberries into the yogurt mixture, being careful not to crush them.

5 Spoon the yogurt mixture into four serving glasses or dishes, top with the remaining raspberries and serve immediately.

6 Pass around a dish of heather honey to drizzle over the top for extra sweetness and flavour.

Per portion Energy 276kcal/1152kJ; Protein 12.4g; Carbohydrate 17.2g, of which sugars 11.1g; Fat 19.7g, of which saturates 8.7g; Cholesterol 0mg; Calcium 255mg; Fibre 2.5g; Sodium 122mg.

strawberry cream shortbreads

These pretty treats are always popular, especially served with afternoon tea or as a quick and easy dessert. Serve them as soon as they are ready because the shortbread cookies will lose their lovely crisp texture if left to stand.

Serves 3

50g/2oz/¼ cup caster (superfine) sugar

115g/4oz/1 cup plain (all-purpose) flour

50g/2oz/scant ⅓ cup ground rice or rice flour

pinch of salt

115g/4oz/½ cup butter

150g/5oz/1¼ cups strawberries

450ml/¾ pint/scant 2 cups double (heavy) cream

Variations

• Two ripe, peeled peaches will also give great results.

• Instead of shortbread, you can use freshly baked scones.

1 Preheat the oven to 190°C/375°F/Gas 5. Line two baking sheets with baking parchment. Put the sugar, flour, ground rice or rice flour and salt in a bowl. Cut the butter into pieces and rub in until the mixture resembles fine breadcrumbs. Mould to a dough with your hands.

2 Lightly roll into a sausage shape, about 7.5cm/3in thick. Using a large, sharp knife, slice the roll into six discs about 1cm/½in thick.

3 Transfer to the baking sheets, and bake for 20–25 minutes until pale golden. Leave to cool for 10 minutes before transferring to a wire rack to cool completely.

4 Reserve three strawberries for decoration. Hull the remaining strawberries and cut them in half. Crush the berries gently using the back of a fork.

5 Put the cream in a large bowl and whip until softly peaking. Add the crushed strawberries and fold in gently, being careful not to mix them too much.

6 Halve the reserved strawberries. Spoon the strawberry and cream mixture on to the shortbreads. Decorate each with half a strawberry and serve immediately.

 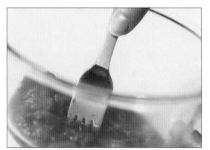 

Per portion Energy 976kcal/4035kJ; Protein 5.7g; Carbohydrate 34.6g, of which sugars 16.8g; Fat 90.8g, of which saturates 50.1g; Cholesterol 206mg; Calcium 122mg; Fibre 1.3g; Sodium 204mg.

clootie dumpling

A rich, dense pudding, traditionally made in a "cloot" or cloth, then boiled over the fire. At the festive season of Hogmanay or New Year a coin is hidden inside.

Serves 8

225g/8oz/2 cups plain (all-purpose) flour, and 15ml/1 tbsp for the cloot
115g/4oz/scant 1 cup suet (US chilled, grated shortening)
115g/4oz/generous 1 cup rolled oats
75g/3oz/scant ½ cup caster (superfine) sugar
5ml/1 tsp baking powder
225g/8oz/generous 1½ cups mixed sultanas (golden raisins) and currants
5ml/1 tsp each ground cinnamon and ground ginger
15ml/1 tbsp golden (light corn) syrup
2 eggs, lightly beaten
45–60ml/3–4 tbsp milk

1 Sift the flour into a dry bowl then add the suet. Rub the fat into the flour until it resembles breadcrumbs. Add the oats, sugar, baking powder, fruit and spices. Mix well then stir in the syrup and eggs, using enough milk to form a firm batter.

2 The cloot should be cotton or linen, about 52cm/21in square. Plunge it into boiling water, remove it from the pan, wring it out and lay it out on a flat surface.

3 Sprinkle 15ml/1 tbsp flour over the cloot. Place the pudding mixture in the middle of the cloth then bring each of the four corners into the middle above the mixture and tie with string, leaving plenty of space for the pudding to expand.

4 Cook for 2½–3 hours by steaming in a double boiler or heat the oven to 150°C/300°F/Gas 2 and place the dumpling in a bain-marie.

5 When cooked, turn on to a large plate. Serve in slices with hot jam and cream.

Variation, if using a heatproof bowl, instead of a cloot

Lightly grease a heatproof bowl and put in the mixture, allowing at least 2.5cm/1in space at the top. Cover with baking parchment and tie down well. Steam in a double boiler for 2½–3 hours over a low heat.

Per portion Energy 902kcal/3798kJ; Protein 15.1g; Carbohydrate 143.3g, of which sugars 69.2g; Fat 35g, of which saturates 16.6g; Cholesterol 121mg; Calcium 183mg; Fibre 5.5g; Sodium 81mg.

drop scones

These popular little bakes are variously known as girdlecakes, griddlecakes and Scotch pancakes. Drop scones make a quick and easy breakfast, elevenses or teatime snack served with butter and drizzled with honey.

Makes 8–10

115g/4oz/1 cup plain (all-purpose)
  flour
5ml/1 tsp bicarbonate of soda
  (baking soda)
5ml/1 tsp cream of tartar
25g/1oz/2 tbsp butter, diced
1 egg, beaten
about 150ml/¼ pint/⅔ cup milk
a knob (pat) of butter and heather
  honey, to serve

Cook's Tip

Placing the cooked scones in a clean folded dish towel will keep them soft and moist. Bring to the table like this and ask your guests to pull them out.

1 Lightly grease a griddle pan or heavy frying pan, then preheat it. Sift the flour, bicarbonate of soda and cream of tartar together into a mixing bowl.

2 Add the diced butter and rub it into the flour with your fingertips until the mixture resembles fine, evenly textured breadcrumbs.

3 Make a well in the centre of the flour mixture, then stir in the egg. Add the milk a little at a time, stirring it in to check consistency. Add enough milk to give a lovely thick creamy consistency.

4 Cook in batches. Drop 3 or 4 evenly sized spoonfuls of the mixture, spaced slightly apart, on the griddle or frying pan. Cook over a medium heat for 2–3 minutes, until bubbles rise to the surface and burst.

5 Turn the scones over carefully and cook for a further 2–3 minutes, until they are golden underneath.

6 Place the cooked scones between the folds of a clean dish towel while cooking the remaining batter. Serve warm, with butter and honey.

Per pancake Energy 90kcal/379kJ; Protein 2.8g; Carbohydrate 12.1g, of which sugars 1.1g; Fat 3.8g, of which saturates 2.1g; Cholesterol 32mg; Calcium 47mg; Fibre 0.5g; Sodium 36mg.

Dundee cake

A classic Scottish fruit cake, this rich cake is made with mixed peel, dried fruit, almonds and spices. It is decorated in the traditional way, covered completely with circles of whole blanched almonds.

Serves 16–20

175g/6oz/¾ cup butter

175g/6oz/¾ cup soft light brown
  sugar

3 eggs

225g/8oz/2 cups plain (all-purpose)
  flour

10ml/2 tsp baking powder

5ml/1 tsp ground cinnamon

2.5ml/½ tsp ground cloves

1.5ml/¼ tsp freshly grated nutmeg

225g/8oz/generous 1½ cups
  sultanas (golden raisins)

175g/6oz/¾ cup glacé (candied)
  cherries

115g/4oz/⅔ cup mixed chopped
  (candied) peel

50g/2oz/½ cup blanched almonds,
  roughly chopped

grated rind of 1 lemon

30ml/2 tbsp brandy

75g/3oz/¾ cup whole blanched
  almonds, to decorate

Variation

Add the grated rind of 1 orange for extra taste and flavour.

1 Preheat the oven to 160°C/325°F/Gas 3. Grease and line a 20cm/8in round, deep cake tin (pan). Cream the butter and sugar together in a large mixing bowl. Add the eggs, one at a time, beating thoroughly after each addition.

2 Sift the flour, baking powder and spices together. Fold into the creamed mixture alternately with the remaining ingredients, apart from the whole almonds. Mix until evenly blended.

3 Transfer the mixture to the tin and smooth the surface, making a dip in the centre.

4 Decorate the top by pressing the almonds in decreasing circles over the entire surface. Bake in the preheated oven for 2–2¼ hours, until a skewer inserted in the centre comes out clean.

5 Cool in the tin for 30 minutes then transfer to a wire rack to cool fully.

Cook's Tip

All rich fruit cakes improve in flavour if left in a cool place for up to 3 months. Wrap the cake in baking parchment and a double layer of foil.

Per portion Energy 321kcal/1347kJ; Protein 4.7g; Carbohydrate 44.2g, of which sugars 33.3g; Fat 14.7g, of which saturates 6.4g; Cholesterol 59mg; Calcium 76mg; Fibre 1.7g; Sodium 107mg.

index